Kippie Moeketsi
Sad man of Jazz

by Peter Esterhuysen

Adapted by Minky Schlesinger
Illustrated by Meg Jordi

BOOKS
Johannesburg

Chapter one

Hard times

The story of Kippie Moeketsi is a sad one. He was
one of the greatest jazz players of his time. But he
ended up without a cent. When he died, in 1983,
his mind was mixed up by drink. His body was
weak. Even his best friends did not want to know
him any more. Kippie was tired of life and gave
up the ghost. He was fifty-eight years old.

Why did the talented Kippie Moeketsi end up in
such a bad way? People say that it all started when
he was a child.

An unhappy little boy

Kippie was born on 27 July 1925 in a slum in the
centre of Johannesburg. His real name was
Jeremiah. He was the fifth son of Zachariah and
Lydia Moeketsi. His older brothers were Jacob,
Samuel, Andrew and Isaiah.

Shortly after Kippie's birth the slum was knocked
down. The Moeketsi family went to live in a small
house in the township of George Goch. Kippie's
father, Zachariah, found work fixing things at the
Jeppestown men's hostel. After a while Kippie's

mother gave birth to a daughter. They called her Miriam, a name they found in the Bible.

Kippie's parents took all their children's names from the Bible because they were churchgoers. Zachariah was a member of the Methodist Church, where he played the organ. The children would listen to old Zach practise the organ in the evenings. They all grew to love music. Kippie and his four brothers all learned to play instruments. When they grew up, the two oldest boys worked as musicians. Jacob, the first-born, became a well-known jazz pianist.

Old Zach was a very strict father. He often fought with Kippie. He got cross when Kippie did not practise his music lessons. Kippie's older brothers used to bully him too. Kippie remembered his childhood with sadness. He once said: 'Life at home was awful. One brother wanted me to learn classical music too fast. He bullied me. My father was

Zach Moeketsi, Kippie's father.

on his side and my mother on mine. But there was little that Mother could do to help me.'

Those were hard times for young Kippie. His father had some harsh ways. One evening Kippie's friend, General Duze, had a meal with the Moeketsi family. He was surprised to see that old Zach's food was served first. Then the whole family waited until the old man had eaten, before they could start. Zach was sometimes quite mean.

Kippie's parents wanted him to be a good scholar. Two of his brothers became teachers. So the

Moeketsis wanted good marks from their youngest son. But Kippie hated school.

Kippie was a rebel. He was more interested in sharp clothing than in school books. He was the last-born of five sons. So when the older boys' clothing was too tight, they passed the clothes down to Kippie. He was forced to wear broken pants and faded shirts. He felt bad to go to school like that. Kippie once said: 'In those days I had no aim in life. I was tired of school life, tired of home life. I was filthy, and in school the mistress often disgraced me in front of everybody.'

It is plain to see that Kippie was a very unhappy little boy. He started to skip classes often. He sold newspapers on the street corner instead of going to George Goch Primary. He and his friends also went to the golf-course to work as caddies. They carried the golfers' bags. But they were paid only a few cents for their work. So they stole golf balls. Then they sold the balls back to the golfers to earn more money.

People say that Kippie sometimes ran off to play in the mine-dumps instead of going to school. Then his mother would hear about it. She would stand on the edge of the dumps and call after him to

Kippie Moeketsi
Sad Man of Jazz

Published by ViVa Books

PO Box 28510, Kensington, 2101, South Africa

First published 1995

Cover illustration by Meg Jordi

ISBN 1 874932 21 2

Acknowledgement
ViVa Books would like to thank Nedbank for their generous contribution towards this book.

Photographic credits
Bailey's African History Archives (opp. page 1, pages 14, 17, 20, 23, 25, 27, 32, 33, 36, 37, 39, 44, 45, 46, 48, 49, 54, 57, 61, 64, 65, 66, 67, 68, 76); Mayibuye Centre (page 50); Jurgen Schadeberg (pages 26, 28, 31, 74); Paul Weinberg (page 70); Zonk magazine - courtesy Bona magazine (pages 2, 3, 7, 10, 15, 22, 46, 60).

Reproduction by Remata Bureau and Printers, Midrand
Printed and bound by Galvin and Sales, Cape Town

come back. But she did not shout his name, 'Jeremiah'. Instead, she yelled after him as if he was a chicken: 'Kippie-kippie-kippie!' That was how Jeremiah Moeketsi became known as 'Kippie'.

A depressed teenager

By the time he was eighteen Kippie had only completed Standard Four. He left school feeling that he had failed. For the rest of his life he was unhappy that he had little schooling. He thought that he was not as good as other people.

Kippie was unable to find a good job because he had so little training. He went to work at a men's hostel as a floor-sweeper. He was bored there, and miserable about the low wages. So he looked for a better job. His next job was at a chemist's shop. He rode a bicycle and carried parcels. By now he was twenty years old and he felt very depressed as a delivery-man.

At that time Kippie's brother Isaiah bought himself a clarinet. Isaiah learned to play the instrument, but he soon got bored with it. He wanted to paint pictures rather than play music. Isaiah passed the clarinet down to Kippie as if it was a pair of pants that were too tight! This was the best gift that anyone ever gave Kippie.

Isaiah painting a picture of himself.

Now Kippie was left alone to play the music he liked. No one bullied him to learn the classics. After work each day Kippie went out into the yard. There he practised the clarinet until the early hours of the morning. The neighbours shouted at him for making a noise. But Kippie did not care. He even taught himself staff notation from a little book that came with the clarinet.

Kippie hoped that Isaiah would teach him to play. But his older brother had no time for him. Whenever Kippie saw Isaiah, he asked, 'Tell me, man, how do I know the clarinet? Where must I put my fingers?'

'*Haai*, no!' Isaiah would shout at him. 'Put your fingers there!'

'What is a crotchet?' Kippie would ask.

Isaiah always got cross. '*Ag* man, you're worrying me,' he would say, 'a crotchet is a beat.'

And that was the end of the lesson.
Kippie tried to copy the music of American jazzmen like Lester Young, Count Basie and Duke

Ellington. He also liked the South African big
band called the Jazz Maniacs. Kippie's brother
Jacob was the pianist for the Jazz Maniacs. The
band was led by Zuluboy Cele until 1944, when he
was murdered by gangsters. As a young boy
Kippie had followed the Jazz
Maniacs all over the
Reef, just to hear

Cele play the
saxophone. Now,
every night, he stood
in his own backyard and
tried to copy his idol.

Life brightens up

George Goch township had a place where
musicians could meet. It was the open square near
the Communal Hall. Many top performers
gathered there for jam sessions. Township folk
crowded around outdoors to hear their favourite
artists. Soon Kippie was joining in. He became
known as a talented clarinet player.

In 1947, when Kippie was twenty-two, he was
asked to join the Band in Blue. This was a new
band. It was formed by Bob Twala. Kippie's
friend and neighbour, General Duze, was invited
to play guitar with them. Life was brightening up!

Kippie decided to leave his delivery job. He spent
all his time on music. He swapped the clarinet for
an alto saxophone. Kippie loved playing this
instrument. Soon he became known as the hottest
young sax player in the township. Kippie found it
easy to learn the sax. 'I didn't practise how to play
the saxophone, I just played it,' Kippie explained.
'*Ja*, once you know a clarinet, a saxophone is a boy!'

Chapter two

Hard work

The Band in Blue

The Band in Blue was a new, young band. They were not famous like the Jazz Maniacs or the Harlem Swingsters. They had to struggle to get gigs in town. Sometimes they performed at a nice place like the Ritz Palais de Danse in Polly Street, or at the Bantu Men's Social Centre. But mostly they played in shebeens, in slum areas around Denver.

Kippie hated these run-down rooms. He called Denver *E-Sidikidikini*, meaning 'the place of hell'. He was upset because the audiences were not interested in music. They came to the shebeens to drink beer and talk. The music was just in the background.

Again, Kippie felt unhappy. The only way he could face these noisy audiences was to drink as much as they did. Kippie was already a dagga-smoker. He thought that dagga helped him to play well. Now he started drinking heavily. Alcohol became a lifelong habit.

The problem of gangsters

Another reason that the Band in Blue could not get work in nice clubs was because of gangsters. During the 1940s and 1950s gangsters controlled the dancehalls. If the thugs did not like a band's music, they stopped the show. Some promoters also employed gangs to break up the concerts staged by their rivals. The worst promoters paid *tsotsis* to injure other musicians.

Often gangsters came to a hall when the concert was finished. Then they forced the band to play some more. Kippie and the Band in Blue sometimes carried on playing until nine o'clock the next morning to please the *tsotsis*.

Many musicians were scared of the gangs. Some musicians carried weapons in their instrument cases so that they could defend themselves. A well-known player even tied a blade to his bass. If you went to a dancehall in those days everyone warned you: 'Bring a knife - not your wife!'

Kippie nearly lost his life many times in those early days. He told this story: 'I remember once when I managed to escape with my dear life. It was in 1948. We were playing at the Bantu Men's Social

Centre. *Tsotsis* came, man! There were about
seventeen, carrying tomahawks and chopping
everybody in the hall for no reason. After they
finished with the audience, they came onto the
stage. We stood glued there, we were so scared.
Then they began chopping up our instruments.
We ran for our lives with the thugs in hot pursuit.

'One of them chased me down Von Wielligh Street. It was about three o'clock in the morning. He shouted at me, "*Kom hier, jong,* Kippie." ... Luckily for me a police van came and the thug ran away.' Kippie was thankful to be alive.

The Harlem Swingsters

In 1949 Kippie and General Duze were invited to join the Harlem Swingsters. This was a great honour because the Swingsters were township heroes.

General Duze, Kippie's friend and neighbour.

The Harlem Swingsters had been going for some time when Kippie joined them. Their leader was

'Taai' Shomang. He played the bass. Other band-members were Benjamin 'Gwigwi' Mrwebi on clarinet; Sylvester 'Skip' Phahlane and Ntemi Piliso on tenor sax; Braggar Ntsoalo on trombone; Todd Matshikiza on piano; and

Norman Martin on drums. After Kippie and General joined up, the Swingsters became a nine-piece orchestra.

As a member of the Swingsters, Kippie did not
have to play in dead-end shebeens. In those days
few black bands performed for white audiences.
But black fans filled up the dancehalls when the
Swingsters put on a show. Their most popular
songs were 'Majuba', 'E-Qonce', and 'Tamatie
Sous'. These were old *marabi* tunes that the
Swingsters played in the jazz style. The audiences
went wild for this new township sound.

Two-band stages

A much-loved event in those days was the
'two-band stage'. This meant that two bands
played at one concert. The two groups took turns
on the stage and competed against each other.
Each band would play more and more wildly to
try and 'outblow' the other band. This was also
known as playing 'two-stage'.

The Swingsters' best concerts were at the Old Jig
Club. There they played two-band stages with the
Jazz Maniacs. After 1944, when Zuluboy Cele was
murdered, the Jazz Maniacs were led by Wilson
'Kingforce' Silgee.

The Swingsters and the Maniacs were the two most
popular bands of the time. Each group had its own

| Wilson 'Kingforce' Silgee, leader of the Jazz Maniacs. | Taai Shomang, leader of the Harlem Swingsters. |

supporters. When they performed together in the same hall the supporters went crazy. Sometimes the fans fought each other with knives, arguing about which was the best orchestra. In those days supporters followed their favourite musicians around, the way soccer fans follow their teams today.

Concert promoters put up posters in the townships. These posters told people where their favourite band was playing.

This is what the posters looked like:

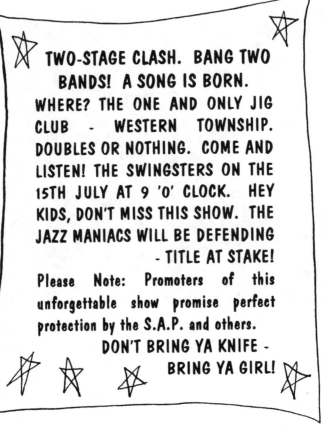

Young people loved the two-band stages. But older folk said it was like going to war!

Life on the road

Most of the big bands spent a lot of time on tour. They travelled all over South Africa, playing for a few days in each town.

Life on the road was not easy for musicians. They missed their families and quarrelled with each other. Sometimes they were arrested for not having passes or because they drank liquor. The police even put artists in jail for making a noise! In those days the cops did not like to see black strangers in their towns. Sometimes the police thought band-members were beggars, so they arrested them.

Even though Kippie enjoyed playing with the Swingsters, he became difficult on tour. Kippie was very moody and small things made him unhappy. He was a man of few words. Sometimes he said nasty things to other musicians. His colleagues never knew what he would do. He often argued with them over nothing.

When Kippie felt someone had wronged him, he did not tell them so. He kept his feelings inside. He worried about it all day. Later on, after he had a few drinks, he got into a bad temper. Nobody understood why Kippie got so cross when he drank. They did not know he was thinking about something that had happened much earlier that day.

The end of the big bands

One thing that caused a lot of fighting amongst musicians was money. It cost a lot to keep a large band together. Usually, the band-leader was in charge of money. Some leaders were dishonest and took more cash for themselves. Other leaders could not look after money well. Every now and then gangsters stole the money taken at the door, and the band did not get paid.

By the early 1950s big bands were starting to break up. The problems of touring and money worries became too much for them.

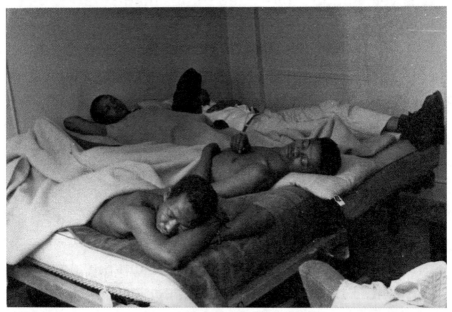

Kippie (in front) shares a room with other musicians on tour. Third from the front is Hugh Masekela.

Chapter three
Sweeter days

Just like the other big bands, the Harlem Swingsters started losing members. Neither Kippie nor General Duze stayed with the group for long. General left in 1950 to join the Rhythm Clouds. He soon found that the Rhythm Clouds fought a lot about money. So General formed his own band. It had only three members. They called it the Shantytown Trio.

The band had General on guitar, Boycie Gwele on piano and Jacob 'Mzala' Lepere on bass. At first, people thought that such a small band was very funny. But even in America the jazz groups were getting smaller. After a few years the big swing orchestras, with twelve or fifteen members, were all gone.

Even so, a band with only three people in it was too small. So the Shantytown Trio started to grow. They became a quartet when Norman Martin joined them on drums. Then Kippie joined and they became a quintet. They ended up with six members when Mackay Davashe, the tenor saxophonist, teamed up with them. They called themselves the Shantytown Sextet. They became very successful.

Mackay Davashe, Kippie, General Duze, Norman Martin, Jacob 'Mzala' Lepere and Boycie Gwele.

The Shantytown Sextet

One of the reasons the Sextet became well known was because of the Manhattan Brothers. The Manhattan Brothers were four vocalists. They had been singing together, in the close-harmony style, since 1935. They were loved in townships all over the country.

The Manhattans' leader, Nathan Dambuza Mdledle, invited the Shantytowners to be their backing band. The two groups worked very well together. So throughout the 1950s the Shantytown Sextet toured with the Manhattan Brothers.

Nathan Dambuza Mdledle, leader of the Manhattan Brothers.

The Manhattan Brothers used to sing in the first half of the concert. They always stopped singing at midnight. After that they let the Sextet play alone. The band played dance music until four in the morning. Audiences came to enjoy the Sextet's music, with or without the Manhattan Brothers!

At last life was becoming sweeter for Kippie. He got on well with the other band-members. He always had money in his pocket. Things were good.

Kippie earned good money from backing the Manhattan Brothers at concerts. But he made money from records too. During the 1950s both the Shantytown Sextet and the Manhattan Brothers put out many hit singles.

Kippie also recorded with other bands. In those days the record companies liked to use 'pickup' groups. These pickup musicians were not a real band. They never played together outside the recording studio. They met in the studio to cut a disc. Today we would call them 'session' musicians. The pickup groups gave themselves clever names. Kippie recorded with the Bee Gee Bees and Kaputnik Jive, as well as many others. His songs were also recorded by the Limelight Boys.

If the record companies had been fair, Kippie would have made a lot of money from his songs. The companies were supposed to pay Kippie royalties on his compositions, for the rest of his life. He would have been a rich man. But, sadly, Kippie never knew that he could claim royalties from the record companies.

All the artists tell the same story. Ntemi Piliso of the African Jazz Pioneers says: 'The companies would pay us five pounds and make us sign for it. They said this would allow them to sell the records. We did not know that we were signing away our royalties.'

Later on, when Kippie was old and poor, he said: 'The record companies are very rich. And I have nothing.' But back in the early 1950s Kippie did not feel too bad. He had enough money for his needs. He was playing with the Shantytown Sextet, and life was going smoothly. But, with Kippie Moeketsi life never stayed smooth for long!

Charlie Parker and bebop

The Shantytown Sextet's music mixed together swing and old township tunes. This style is known as Township Jazz. But, one day, General Duze came home with a new record from America. It was a record of Charlie 'Bird' Parker and his band. Parker, who played alto sax, and other American jazzmen had made a brand new sound. They called it 'bebop'.

Kippie already knew this sound from the records of Dizzy Gillespie and Thelonious Monk. Even in earlier days, with the Harlem Swingsters, he had tried out a bit of bop. The other Swingsters used to say that he was not playing real music. Band-member Skip Phahlane said that Kippie's fingers moving up and down the saxophone were like 'rolling stones'. Kippie's nickname, 'Morolong', grew out of those words. But Kippie turned the name upside down. Kippie started calling everyone else

'Morolong'! He carried on calling people 'Morolong' throughout his life.

Kippie liked bebop even before he heard Charlie Parker's record. But when he heard Charlie Parker on sax, he could not believe his ears. Kippie was surprised that Parker's playing was so quick and clean. He practised daily to copy that sound. General says that Kippie picked up the style quickly. 'He was like that. He could take any kind of music and do things with it on the sax.'

Now that Kippie was a member of the Shantytown Sextet he wanted to play bebop. But the other members of the group were not practising the new style. This caused some problems. General Duze tells this story: 'During one of our Cape Town tours the band was staying in Langa. There was a guy who had just come

General Duze.

back from America. He showed us some new chord sequences. Then we sat down and played blues songs like "Lady Be Good", sax solos and all.

Kippie wrote down the solo he had just played. Then he turned this solo into a whole new tune.

'We never told the other musicians. They were out at parties or playing cards somewhere. Then, during concerts, the other members would have difficulty with Kippie's solos. Mackay Davashe was now the leader of the Sextet. He would say: "What's happening? These guys aren't playing out of key!" He didn't realize that we were progressing with bop!'

Kleintjie Rubushe, Mackay Davashe and Kippie play at a township dance.

Kippie thought that Charlie Parker and bebop were great. But Kippie had his own special talent. His musical style did not come only from Charlie Parker and America. Kippie enjoyed South African jazz players, too. So Kippie hated it when everyone said he was just like Charlie Parker. He got angry when people asked him to play Charlie Parker songs all the time.

People who did not like Kippie said that Kippie copied his music and his way of life from Charlie Parker. The two musicians were very much the same, even though they never met each other. Both of them were sensitive and touchy: they got into bad moods easily. They both lived on alcohol and drugs. They were both very clever. They did not like stupid people. Both Kippie and Charlie Parker played jazz as if they were born with saxophones in their hands.

When Charlie Parker dropped dead in America, in 1955, he was only thirty-four years old. He died from alcohol and drugs. People said that Parker's soul lived on inside Kippie Moeketsi.

The 'King's Holiday'

In 1957 the Manhattan Brothers and the Shantytown Sextet toured the Cape. By that time

people had seen these groups many times before. They were bored with the show. At the first concert the audience did not want to hear all the same old songs. They became wild and smashed the hall.

After that, the Manhattans and the Sextet played to small audiences.

The pianist, Todd Matshikiza, was unhappy about the tour. So he left the band. Dambuza Mdledle, the Manhattans' leader, looked everywhere for another pianist. One day he brought a young man to meet the group.

Todd Matshikiza, pianist for the Shantytown Sextet.

Newspapers reported that this pianist's name was Adolph Botha, but everyone called him Dollar Brand.

Dambuza went up to Kippie. He asked Kippie: 'Do you know this guy?' and he pointed to Dollar.

'*Ja*,' Kippie answered, 'this guy I know ... I saw him once at Rio bioscope in Johannesburg. He played with me at a concert. *Ja*, I know this boy.' Dollar was still young at that time.

'Can he play piano?' asked Dambuza.

'I think he is capable,' Kippie replied.

'Okay, let's take him,' Dambuza said. Dollar was

Dollar Brand.

so scared of all the older musicians that he could hardly stand up.

In later years, Kippie laughed when he remembered that day. He told a journalist: 'Dollar was kneeling down, nearly begging us, man. I'm telling you. This Dollar Brand - things do happen, s'true's God!'

Dambuza gave Dollar the job. He played piano for the Sextet for the rest of the tour. Dollar was a quiet young man in his early twenties. He was tall and thin, and he always wore a huge pair of boots. Just like Kippie, Dollar was serious about music. He also loved the bebop style. The two men became close friends. Dollar said that Kippie was like a musical father to him.

The Shantytown Sextet saw that Cape audiences did not like their music. So they left Cape Town and went to Port Elizabeth. They took Dollar with them. The Sextet tried out a new kind of music when they got to Port Elizabeth. This is how Kippie explained it: 'We said that we are not going to play English music

Dollar plays the piano while Kippie shares a cigarette.

any more. We are going to play indigenous music - Xhosa, Sesotho and all that. We did change, *ja*. We could read and write music, but we were doing it all by ear - quickly. African music is easy. We didn't write it down. We just wrote the tune, that's all. Afterwards we arranged it our own way.'

The Port Elizabeth audiences went crazy for this new music. People from all over the Eastern Cape invited the Sextet to put on shows. For the next few months the group toured everywhere in the Eastern Cape. They earned good money and spent it quickly. They called the tour the 'King's Holiday' because they lived like kings.

To tell the truth, the group spent every cent they earned. When they got to Queenstown they were broke again. Dambuza wanted to tour some more. But Kippie was fed up. He wanted to go home. Dambuza would not give the band-members their train tickets home. So Kippie became furious. On stage that night Kippie got even in true Kippie style. While Dambuza was singing their hit song, 'Kilimanjaro', Kippie urinated on Dambuza's pants! Kippie shouted: 'Dambuza, I want to go home!'

The tour came to a sudden end. The Sextet went back to Johannesburg. Dollar went home to Cape Town to continue his education. The 'King's Holiday' was over.

Chapter four

The best years

From the middle of the 1950s to the early 1960s were the best years of Kippie's career. He was now in his thirties. He was a highly respected alto player. His records were big sellers. Other bands invited him to play with them because he pulled in the crowds. Kippie always had somewhere to perform. Luckily, new jazz clubs had opened up.

New venues for black artists

In 1955 the Modern Jazz Club organized some concerts. They held the shows on Sunday afternoons at the Odin Cinema in Sophiatown. The Odin was a smart cinema. Middle-class people used to go there. Soon, white jazz players joined in the gigs. In those days it was against the law for blacks and whites to be on a stage together. The Odin became a meeting place for musicians of all races.

Kippie enjoyed playing at the Odin. At last he had interested audiences: they were all jazz lovers. He could play bebop and no one would scorn him. He was always popular at the Odin. Kippie was friendly with many young musicians. He invited them to play with him. He introduced Hugh Masekela and Jonas

Hugh Masekela.

Gwangwa to 'Jazz at the Odin'. When Dollar Brand gave up his studies and moved to Johannesburg, Kippie took him along too.

Concerts were also organized by Union Artists. This was the first union to look after black entertainers. Union Artists, who were based at Dorkay House, held training courses and jazz competitions. They also put on shows at the Selborne Hall in Johannesburg and at the Bantu Men's Social Centre. They called them the

'Township Jazz' and the 'Dorkay Jazz' concerts. There were special days when whites came to see the shows.

In those days white people and black people could not sit in the same audience. Often, performers from overseas played for white fans only. Union Artists demanded that visiting artists put on shows for black music lovers, too.

Tony Scott.

In 1957, a famous American clarinettist named Tony Scott came to Johannesburg. He was very unhappy that whites and blacks were in separate audiences. So he insisted on doing a mixed concert. He appeared at the Wits University Great Hall, where everyone could attend. But blacks had to sit on one side, while whites sat on the other side. Tony Scott did not like this. He showed how angry he was by breaking the law: he appeared on the stage with a black musician. From all the local players, he chose Kippie Moeketsi.

Tony Scott thought that Kippie was great. He said: 'If Kippie Moeketsi could be trained overseas and get experience in the United States, he would be one of the finest players in the world.'

When Scott went home, he promised to try and raise money overseas. He wanted to send Kippie and the Durban pianist, Lionel Pillay, to America. Some time later Scott sent Kippie a present of a new clarinet. But nothing came of his other promises. Kippie's life was full of broken promises.

There were some good things that came from mixing with white musicians. Kippie and other black artists were invited to play in white hotels. They got gigs in white restaurants. Some got jobs at parties in white suburbs. The Montparnasse Coffee Bar, in Hillbrow, made Wednesday nights a platform for black jazz. Another Johannesburg hotel started the Progressive Jazz Club.

For Kippie, playing at small venues was a blessing. When Kippie performed in large township halls he had to play a bit of *mbaqanga*. Otherwise the crowd got angry. Kippie did not really like *mbaqanga*. In smaller venues, the audiences were true jazz fans. So Kippie could play the modern jazz he loved.

One of the best modern jazz groups in the country grew out of the jazz evenings at small clubs. The group was called the Jazz Epistles.

The Jazz Epistles

The Jazz Epistles had Kippie on alto saxophone; Dollar Brand on piano; Hugh Masekela on trumpet; Jonas Gwangwa on trombone; Johnny Gertze on guitar; and Makhaya Ntshoko on drums. Kippie said that the Jazz Epistles was the best band he ever played with.

The Jazz Epistles were so good that white jazz lovers demanded to hear them. But, by the later 1950s, the apartheid laws were squeezing black entertainers. Now, when the Epistles played at white bars and hotels, they were forced to enter

through the back door. The band could not sit in the club during breaks. They had to wait in the kitchen.

One evening the Jazz Epistles were playing in a Johannesburg nightclub. When they took a break, the owner led them to the kitchen. He gave the musicians a meal. Then he went back inside his club. While the Epistles were eating, Kippie became very cross. He said: 'By right, you know Dollar, this is all nonsense - this idea of us being taken into the kitchen when there's a break. Are we "kitchen boys"? Aren't we here to entertain the people?'

'*Ja, ou pellie,*' Dollar answered, '*ons kom nou en dan by die kombuis* ... the scullery department.' Kippie started to make up a new song right there in the kitchen. He called his new song 'Scullery Department'.

The group decided to protest. They called the son of the nightclub owner into the kitchen. 'Look, *pellie,*' they told him, 'it is not good this thing of you bringing us into the kitchen for our meal. You better see that we get our own table, right there among the customers. We are also important here, you know? In fact, we ARE the thing here! If it were not for us, you would have no customers.'

'But guys, I will lose my licence!' the owner's son said.

'Your licence?' the Epistles answered. 'Then why do they let us play in front of whites, if we cannot eat together?'

The owner's son went away. After a few minutes he called the band into the club. He had set a table for them among the customers. The Epistles never went back into that hotel kitchen again.

The Epistles recorded 'Scullery Department' on their first album. It was one of the finest songs that Kippie ever wrote.

Kippie's private life

Kippie was a sensitive person. He was very hurt when people treated him like a 'kitchen boy'. Even though his work was going well, he was not a happy man. He never felt easy inside his own skin. He was still drinking heavily and smoking dagga. Some magazines wrote that Kippie had started to use stronger drugs too.

Kippie never married. But he did have a girlfriend named Becky. They had two children together. But Kippie was not always proud of her. He sometimes wished for a well-educated woman. He said, 'The intellectual girl won't let you down at gatherings. She knows how to handle you.'

Kippie was not easy to live with. He was often tense or depressed. Can Themba wrote in *Drum Magazine*: 'Kippie Moeketsi lives on tension. He is so high-strung that while he is talking to you, you might believe that he is twanging, like a guitar.'

Even Kippie's friends did not know how to handle him. Ntemi Piliso says: 'When Kippie was sober he was a hell of a nice guy. He had a very sharp mind. And he was not selfish. He was always happy to share his knowledge of music.' But, every now and then, Kippie fought with his friends for no reason.

44

Ntemi Piliso plays with Kippie.

Ntemi remembers that he once spent a happy morning with Kippie, at a place called 'Loafer's Corner'. They had a few drinks. Then Ntemi went to the recording studio. When he came back later that day, Kippie was in a bad temper. He screamed at Ntemi: 'You think you are so smart in your fancy clothes. I'll just bust you up!'

When Kippie was drunk he often said he would bust people up. Sometimes when other musicians performed, Kippie shouted: 'You. You think you play jazz? You don't play jazz, you play rubbish! Watch this ...' Then Kippie played his sax, to show them how to do it. Kippie was always starting fights with other musicians. But usually he was the one who got beaten up. Ntemi remembers that Kippie once said something ugly to the drummer, Early Mabuza. Early nearly killed Kippie that day.

Kippie was never content. He did not like playing in township halls. But he also did not like white audiences. In 1961 he told a *Drum Magazine* journalist: 'You play nonsense overseas and they tell you it is nonsense. Here they say it is nice. Isn't Kippie clever? Isn't Kippie cute? In the

townships they don't want to hear me, they want to dance. In the white clubs they eat while I play. They all come to enjoy themselves, not to hear me. I call them monkeys, baboons.'

Even during the most successful years of Kippie's life, he was not a happy man.

Chapter five

King Kong

In 1960 Kippie got a chance to go
overseas. He went with the musical
show, *King Kong*. But the trip ended
badly for him. This is the whole
sad story.

Ezekiel Dhlamini

The musical, *King Kong*, was the
story of a real boxer. His name
was Ezekiel Dhlamini. Dhlamini
was a heavyweight champ. He
was a township hero: people said no
one would ever beat him. Everyone
called Dhlamini 'King Kong',
because he was as strong as a gorilla.

Then Dhlamini lost a boxing match
against a middleweight fighter.
Nobody could believe it! This fight
ended his career. After that he
became very violent. One night, at a
dancehall, he stabbed his girlfriend
to death.

At his trial Dhlamini pleaded guilty. He asked the judge for the death sentence. He did not want to live any more. But the judge sent him to jail. In 1957, Dhlamini escaped from prison. He went straight to a nearby dam and drowned himself.

Soon afterwards, a lawyer named Harry Bloom wrote a play about Dhlamini. He asked Todd Matshikiza to compose the music. But Todd was playing with Kippie and the Shantytown Sextet in Cape Town. That was the tour when audiences did not support the Sextet and Todd was unhappy. Todd left the band. He went straight back to Johannesburg to write the songs for *King Kong*.

Busy days

A young man named Stanley 'Spike' Glasser was in charge of the music for *King Kong*. He had to form a band for the show. He chose the best players from all the big bands. He put together a fourteen-piece orchestra. The band had Mackay Davashe and Skip Phahlane on tenor sax; Kippie on alto sax; Gwigwi Mrwebi on clarinet; Jonas Gwangwa and Dugmore Slinger on trombone; Simon Chose, Joseph 'Kleintjie' Rubushe and Hugh Masekela on trumpet; Sol Klaaste on piano; Mzala

Lepere on bass; Ben Maoela on drums; and General
Duze on guitar. The band was called the Jazz
Dazzlers.

In September 1958, Spike Glasser asked Kippie,
Mackay Davashe and Sol Klaaste to help him
arrange the music. The play was going to open in
February 1959. They had five months to prepare.
Now Kippie's days were very busy. In the
mornings Mackay, Sol and Kippie met at Spike's
house to work on the songs. After lunch they
rushed into town to practise with the band. Then
at six o'clock they rehearsed with the actors.

**Mackay Davashe and Spike Glasser talk about the
music for King Kong.**

Rehearsals often carried on until the early hours of the morning. Sometimes, after rehearsals, Kippie, Mackay and Sol went back to Spike Glasser's house to work some more. Kippie explained: 'At times we would go back to Glasser's home in Orange Grove or Yeoville, spend some nights there. Or go home at about three o'clock in the morning - with a bottle of whisky. This was to keep stimulating us.' Towards the end Kippie, Mackay, Sol and Spike worked right through the nights.

American jazz pianist John Mehegan, who visited South Africa in 1959, shares ideas with Kippie.

In January 1959 the producers of *King Kong* decided to make a record of the music from the show. They wanted to sell this record at the first performance. So Kippie and the others had to record fourteen tracks in less than two weeks. The musicians and cast were very busy. But by 2 February everything was ready.

A scene from King Kong. The man sitting on the cart is Dan Poho.

A smash hit!

The play opened at the Wits University Great Hall and was a huge success. For many whites, this was their first taste of township life. They loved the story and the dancing. But, most of all, they loved the music.

Kippie and the rest of the band sat in the orchestra pit. This is a special place for the band in front of the stage. It is lower than the audience. So the orchestra and the public cannot see each other. At the end of the first performance the musicians were surprised to hear loud clapping. Then a large crowd rushed down to the orchestra pit to watch them play. The band was very pleased.

Eight days after *King Kong* opened, all performances were sold out. The play toured to Cape Town, Durban and Port Elizabeth and then returned to Johannesburg for a second run. The 'SOLD OUT' sign went up in every town. *King Kong* was a smash hit.

Life in the orchestra pit went smoothly. The musicians became close friends. They could sit back and enjoy themselves because the audience could not see them. It got very hot in the pit. So the musicians took off their shirts. Then they brought out bread and fish and chips. Playing in *King Kong* was like playing in your own backyard.

The producers were worried about discipline in the cast. They were especially worried about Kippie Moeketsi. They knew all about Kippie's bad habits. They told Gwigwi Mrwebi to keep an eye on him. But Kippie surprised everyone and caused no trouble. In fact, it was the other musicians who played a trick on Kippie, when they got to Durban.

There had been heavy floods in Durban that year. The musicians decided to use this to play a joke on Kippie. Every night in the orchestra pit, the musicians would all jog their knees up and down and make the floor of the pit shake. Then they told Kippie the floor was shaking because the building was not strong. They said that the heavy rains had made the theatre weak. Kippie worried all the time that the place would fall down on them. The other musicians had a good laugh.

King Kong played all over the country for eight months. Then the cast got the big news: they were going to London!

King Kong goes to London

On 7 February 1961 the cast of *King Kong* flew to London. But Kippie was not with them. He was lying in hospital with a fractured skull.

Some people say that *tsotsis* beat Kippie up because they were jealous of him. But other people tell a different story. Before leaving for London, they say, Kippie went home to say goodbye to his girlfriend, Becky. Becky's father was waiting for him. The old man was cross because Kippie and Becky were not yet married. The two men got into a fight and Kippie was hit on the head. Kippie ended up in hospital.

After two weeks of treatment, Kippie joined the cast in London. But he felt bad in this foreign country. He was not used to talking to rich people. Kippie was very tense. He started to hit the bottle again. And when he got drunk he became rude

Kippie and Kleintjie Rubushe sign autographs in London.

and noisy. He wanted to fight with everybody.
The other cast-members could not discipline him.

After one week in London, Kippie was put into a
mental hospital. Everyone thought that he was
still mixed up because of his head injury. The
doctors in the hospital gave Kippie electric shock
treatment. They said that his love of music was
making him mad.

After a few weeks one of the doctors took Kippie to
a jazz concert. Oscar Peterson and his Trio came
onto the stage. Kippie got very excited. When
they started to play, Kippie
jumped up on his seat.
The doctor shouted
at him to sit
down.

Then it was Ella Fitzgerald's turn to sing. Kippie jumped up on his seat again. He could not keep still. 'No, Kippie,' the doctor said, 'you are not all right yet. You must stay in the hospital for a while.'

When Kippie seemed better he came out of the mental home. But he kept getting into trouble in London. One evening he was at a well-known jazz club. A famous musician called Tubby Hayes was playing there. Kippie was drunk. This is what Kippie said about that night: 'I met Tubby when I was drunk. I even fought him. Tubby was playing, you see. He stimulated me. I wanted to play. But he didn't want me to play at all. I was mad. I got up there and started to play. But I was not yet myself. You know, you've got to get up there. Then get the mood, the feel of it.'

Kippie was very unhappy in London. He got into many fights. No one could control him. So the producers sent him back to South Africa. After just one and a half months in London, Kippie came home.

King Kong was not as successful overseas as it had been at home. But the cast did perform there until the end of 1961. Then they returned home. But

fifteen performers did not return to South Africa. They went into exile and made new lives for themselves in London. The rest of the cast came back in time for Christmas.

Kippie Moeketsi had already been back for months. He blamed his head injury for his bad moods in London. He said the knock on his head had messed up his memory and his balance. But most people say that Kippie was ruined by drink.

Chapter six

The beginning of the end

The 1960s were difficult times for black people in South Africa. The apartheid laws became more and more strict. Sophiatown had been knocked down because of the Group Areas Act. This was very bad for jazz musicians. The Odin Cinema, where they used to play, was now gone. The Modern Jazz Club was no more.

In 1961, sixty-seven people were shot dead in Sharpeville at a protest against passes. After that the laws got even stricter. Blacks and whites were not allowed to mix together at all. The multiracial jazz clubs closed down. Now there were few places where musicians could earn a living.

Another problem was Radio Bantu. Radio Bantu started in 1961. The disc jockeys on Radio Bantu played very little jazz. They broadcast mainly *mbaqanga*, and the public began to enjoy this music more than jazz. The people who ran Radio Bantu were also very strict about the words on records. If they did not like the words they scratched the discs with blades. Then the disc jockeys could not play them.

South African jazz was under attack. For some musicians, it was the beginning of the end.

Kippie plays with many different bands

After he came back from London, Kippie played with many different bands. His beloved Jazz Epistles had broken up. Hugh Masekela got a scholarship to study in America, and Dollar Brand went back to Cape Town. Kippie was very upset. But he joined up with the Gideon Nxumalo Quintet. This group mixed traditional music with jazz.

When the Jazz Dazzlers came back from the *King Kong* tour of England, Kippie teamed up with them again. They became a seven-piece orchestra and called themselves the New Jazz Dazzlers. Their biggest audiences were at large jazz festivals.

The jazz festivals

A new style of jazz concert started in the 1960s. These were outdoor festivals in large stadiums. The best one took place in 1962 at the Moroka-Jabavu Stadium. It was called the Cold Castle Jazz Festival and it was sponsored by South

African Breweries. Three thousand people attended. The New Jazz Dazzlers won first prize: a contract to perform all over South Africa. It was worth three thousand rands.

The New Jazz Dazzlers. Kippie is on the left.

On 7 September 1963 there was another Cold Castle Jazz Festival. Thousands of fans gathered at Orlando Stadium. But this time the festival went badly wrong. At times the stage lights went out. At other times the loudspeakers did not work. The musicians could not be heard above the noise of the crowd. The crowd became drunk and violent. There were fights and open sex all over the stadium.

At this festival people did not support the New Jazz Dazzlers. They wanted to hear *mbaqanga*. Kippie was very depressed. He felt sick about all the fighting and lovemaking at the festival. And he was sad that the audience did not enjoy his music. He said that he would never take part in a jazz festival again.

The next year's jazz festival, in 1964, was the biggest event of all. More than twenty thousand people attended. But the festival ended in death. Again, there was much drinking and fighting. But this time people were killed. The sponsors said that they would not give money to any more festivals. The music scene in South Africa had turned sour.

Dollar Brand leaves South Africa

Like Kippie, Dollar Brand was very depressed. The apartheid laws were causing a lot of suffering. The police never left black people alone. There was no work for musicians and no money.

And the fans did not care about jazz. Dollar decided to try his luck overseas.

Kippie was deeply unhappy to lose his old friend. He went down to Cape Town to join Dollar for a farewell concert. The day that Dollar's train left for Johannesburg, Kippie, Early Mabuza, Pung Arendse and Dollar drank many bottles of sweet white wine together. By the time Dollar got to the station the train was already leaving. If he missed the train he would miss his flight from Jan Smuts Airport! Dollar quickly jumped on. Kippie just stood and watched him go. Another great musician had gone into exile.

Kippie hits the skids

Right through the 1960s Kippie went from bad to worse. He drank heavily and used even more drugs. He became so rude when he was drunk that many shebeens banned him. He spent most of his time at the George Goch Beerhall, often causing fights.

Promoters could not trust Kippie any more. So he got fewer jobs. Even his musician friends got cross with him. He was always asking them for money, saying, 'Morolong, the kids are hungry.' When Kippie's cash ran out he pawned his saxophone. Then someone would lend him money to get it back.

Kippie appeared at concerts dead drunk. Sometimes he could not even stand up properly. He got onto the stage on his knees, with his sax swinging over his shoulder.

People came to the shows to see the funny things
Kippie did. They were less and less interested in
his music.

As a young man Kippie had felt that audiences
never respected him enough. He played the
saxophone like nobody else. He put his heart and
soul into the music. Yet people talked and laughed
while he performed. Now that he was older,
Kippie went crazy when the fans did not show
respect.

One day, at a party in Hillbrow, some students started clapping and shouting in time to Kippie's music. Kippie was so cross that he hit them with his saxophone. The other musicians had to hold him back. Afterwards Kippie said: 'Why play for people who don't listen? That's why I let them have it with my horn!'

By the late 1960s Kippie had left his girlfriend and children. He was staying with his old mother in Soweto. He was semi-retired, playing a few gigs now and then to earn a couple of rands. He was in his forties but he looked much older than that. He had little money and his clothes were broken. Some people thought he was a beggar. Other people thought that he was completely mad.

The 1970s

The 1970s were no better for Kippie. His mother
was now blind and ill. Kippie was worried that he
would be 'thrown into a hostel' when his mother
died. He spoke of trying to find a wife, but he had
left it a bit late. No woman wanted a drunken
Kippie Moeketsi for a husband.

Every now and then a newspaper reported that a businessman or a sponsor was raising money for Kippie to go overseas. People still thought that Kippie should join Dollar Brand and Hugh Masekela. But all the money-raising came to nothing.

Kippie still performed once in a while. The Soul Brothers respected Kippie and felt sorry for him. They invited him to join their concerts. But, before long, music critics complained that 'a top alto player' was spoiling all their shows. Many musicians felt they could no longer work with Kippie. They banned him from their gigs.

One good thing about the 1970s was the records that Kippie made. He cut records with Barney Rachabane, Allan Kwela and Victor Ntoni. He even had a hit single with pianist Pat Matshikiza and saxophonist Basil 'Manenburg' Coetzee. It was called 'Tshona'. During this time Kippie also made one of the finest records of his career. The album was called 'Dollar Brand + 3 with Kippie Moeketsi'. It was recorded in the early 1970s, when Dollar came home for a while. Dollar staged some shows in Soweto and Kippie appeared as a guest artist.

But the friendship between Kippie and Dollar was not the same. Dollar had taken the Muslim faith a few years before. He now called himself Abdullah Ibrahim. Muslims do not drink and take drugs. So Kippie's habits made Dollar very sad. Kippie and Dollar quarrelled all the time.

In 1977 Kippie had had enough. He said that he was retiring from music. He went to stay in Garankuwa with the famous jazz singer Dolly Rathebe. Dolly was Kippie's cousin. She was also not performing at that time.

For the next five years Kippie played no music.

Chapter seven
Go well, Kippie

In 1982, a woman named Queeneth Ndaba formed a big band. Queeneth was a dress designer and show promoter. Her office was in Dorkay House. Many old musicians gathered at Dorkay House because Union Artists' training courses and concerts had been held there for many years. Dorkay House was the home of black music during the 1960s and 70s.

Queeneth felt sorry for the older jazz players. She also saw that things were changing in South Africa. Now people wanted to know more about Sophiatown and the history of this country. So Queeneth formed a big band to remind people about the township jazz of the 1950s. She invited Kippie to join them. The other musicians in the band protested, because of Kippie's bad name. But Queeneth insisted. The band called themselves the African Jazz Pioneers. They went on to become very popular.

Sadly, Kippie was only half the musician he used to be. But he still had a lot of power. He was also

drinking less because his health was failing. Many people said that Kippie became softer as he got older.

There was still one thing that made Kippie furious. That was the South African music industry. All through his life Kippie felt that the industry had cheated him. Many years before, he told a white promoter: 'You white boy, you can't sing, you can't dance, you can't play a musical instrument and yet you get all the money!' Kippie felt angry about this until the day he died.

In his last year Kippie formed a working friendship with a young white musician. His name was Steve Kuny. Steve met Kippie at one of the Jazz Pioneers' gigs. And Kippie invited Steve to play with the band as a guest artist.

Kippie and Steve played together in a few concerts. They also jammed inside the Market Theatre. They passed a hat around for money at the end. The two musicians began to speak about starting a new band.

But this never happened. In 1983, Kippie gave up the struggle to stay alive.

One Sunday afternoon the African Jazz Pioneers were doing a television show. Kippie and the other band-members drank a little whisky during the break. When they started to play again, Ntemi Piliso noticed that Kippie looked tired and sick. In fact, Kippie had had a chest illness for some time.

On the following Tuesday Kippie did not pitch up at rehearsals. He was now staying with his sister, and she had taken him to the hospital. On Wednesday night, while the rest of the Jazz Pioneers were playing at the Soweto Homemakers' Festival, Kippie died. He was fifty-eight years old.

Kippie was buried on the following Saturday. The funeral service was held at the Eyethu Cinema in Mofolo. It was a huge event. More than two thousand people attended. The funeral went on for three hours and many top singers and musicians made speeches praising Kippie.

In the middle of the service Kippie's old friend, General Duze, left. He went and got drunk. He felt that the funeral was like a circus. He said: 'They were saying all those beautiful, flowery things about Kippie that weren't true. He was a man who had his faults like the rest of us. When Kippie was alive nobody wanted him - now that he is dead everyone has so much to say.'

Kippie's funeral procession. Ntemi Piliso stands on the right. Dolly Rathebe and Tandie Klaasen sit in front.

Kippie knew this was going to happen. In 1968 he told a journalist: 'Spiritually I am dead. My own friends hate me now. They have banned me from the stage, and I hardly have a decent pair of trousers and a shirt. Today I no longer exist as far as the critics are concerned. But watch the great words they will write about me when I am dead. They will say: "He was certainly the greatest ... the world's best, drunk or sober." Only when I am dead.'

It is quite true that Kippie's story has lived on long past his death. These days people talk about Kippie as a 'jazz genius'. Many younger players try to get hold of Kippie's old records, to try and learn his style. He is written about in books and magazines. In March 1987 a new jazz venue opened at the Market Theatre. This club is called 'Kippie's'.

Kippie Moeketsi led a sad life, a stormy life. Storms can be frightening and the rain can make us feel depressed. But rain fills up the rivers and makes everything grow. Kippie's work helped a truly South African music to take root. His influence hangs over our music like a thundercloud.

Some of Kippie's records

It is not easy to find out how many records Kippie made. The record companies did not always give credit to all the musicians. Kippie played alto sax or clarinet on many records by the Manhattan Brothers, the Shantytown Sextet and the Harlem Swingsters. These are just a few of his records:

78s

The Bee Gee Bees - BB 2009.
Kippie and his Marabi Kings - USA 60.
Kaputnik Jive - Quality TJ 193.
'Ekuseni' - Kippie Moeketsi - USA 37.
Dueb Jive Kings - Quality TJ 160.

Extended 45s

'King of the Alto Sax' - Rave 29.

Long players

'King Kong' - Various - GALP 1040.
'Jazz in Africa' - Various - Gallo Continental 9.
'Jazz Epistles, Verse One' - Jazz Epistles - Gallo
                Continental 14.
'King Kong' (Second Version) - Various - GALP 1133.

'Jazz Fantasia' - Gideon Nxumalo Quintet.

'1962 Cold Castle Jazz Festival' - Various - Gallo NSL 1010.

'Jazz, the African Sound' - Chris McGregor's Cold Castle Band - NSL 1011.

'Dollar Brand + 3 with Kippie Moeketsi' - Dollar Brand and Kippie Moeketsi - Gallo/Soultown 113.

'Tshona' - Pat Matshikiza and Kippie Moeketsi - GL 1796.

'Black Lightning' - Dollar Brand - SRK 786138.

'Blue Stompin'' - Kippie Moeketsi and Hal Singer - GL 1912.

Word list

arrange (pages 34, 48) - planned how to play it

artists (pages 9, 19, 24 ...) - people who make music, act or dance for an audience

backing band (page 23) - band that plays for a singing group

balance (page 57) - ability to stand up straight and walk properly

bioscope (page 31) - movie-house

broadcast (page 58) - played over the radio

bully (page 3) - pick on him

capable (page 31) - able to do it

career (pages 35, 46, 68) - working life

chord sequences (page 27) - groups of notes played in a pattern

classical music (page 3), **the classics** (page 7) - very old music, written by people overseas

close-harmony style (page 22) - a way of singing in which people take different parts and harmonize

compositions (page 24) - songs that he wrote

content (page 45) - satisfied and happy

contract (page 60) - legal agreement

crotchet (page 8) - a musical note

depressed (pages 6, 43, 61, 74) - unhappy

disgraced (page 4) - shamed

electric shock treatment (page 55) - a treatment for mad people: the doctor gives them shocks to try and make them better

entertainers (pages 36, 40) - people who sing or act for an audience

fed up (page 34) - tired of doing the same thing

fractured skull (page 54) - a broken head

furious (pages 43, 70) - very angry

gave up the ghost (page 1) - died

gigs (pages 11, 35, 38 ...) - jobs playing music

high-strung (page 43) - nervous and easily upset

hit the bottle (page 54) - to drink heavily

hits the skids (page 62) - loses control of his drinking

idol (page 9) - hero

in hot pursuit (page 13) - chasing after him

influence (page 74) - the power to change the way that other musicians play

injury (pages 55, 57) - wound

instrument (pages 2, 7, 10 ...) - guitars, trumpets, pianos and other things for making music

intellectual (page 43) - well-schooled, clever

Ja, ou pellie, ons kom nou en dan by die kombuis (page 42) - Yes, old pal, now and then we end up in the kitchen

jam sessions (page 9), **jammed** (page 48) - playing music together without practising

journalist (pages 32, 45, 73) - a person who writes for a newspaper or magazine

Kom hier, jong (page 14) - come here, man

loafer (page 44) - a lazy person

mbaqangu (pages 39, 58, 61) - popular dance music

mental hospital (page 55) - a hospital for mad people

miserable (page 6) - sad

moody (page 19) - short-tempered

music critics (page 67) - people who write about music

music industry (page 70) - all the people in the music business

orchestra (pages 15, 17, 21 ...) - band

out of key (page 28) - not in tune

pawned (page 63) - gave to a shop who kept it in exchange for money

performers (pages 9, 37, 56) - people who make music, act or dance for an audience

pleaded guilty (page 47) - admitted his crime

producers (pages 49, 53, 56) - managers of the show

promoters (pages 12, 17, 63 ...) - people who organize and put up the money for a concert

quarrelled (pages 19, 68) - fought

rebel (page 4) - a person who does things differently from everyone else

rehearsed (page 48) - practised for the show

retiring (page 68) - giving up

royalties (pages 24, 25) - money paid to an artist for each record sold

scholarship (page 59) - money to study overseas

scorn (page 36) - mock

scullery department (page 42) - kitchen

semi-retired (page 62) - working every now and then

sensitive (pages 29, 43) - easily hurt

solos (pages 19, 28) - parts of the song where a jazz musician plays alone and makes up the music as he goes

spiritually (page 73) - in his soul

staff notation (page 5) - a way of writing down music

stimulating (page 49) - inspiring, giving us good ideas

swing (pages 21, 26) - a style of jazz played by large bands during the 1930s

tense (pages 43, 54) - very nervous

tomahawks (page 13) - big axes

traditional (page 59) - African music

tsotsis (pages 12, 13, 54) - gangsters

upside down (page 26) - the wrong way round

urinated (page 34) - to go to the toilet and release waste liquid from your body

venues (pages 35, 39) - places where music is played

vocalists (page 22) - singers